How to Manage Your

ECO-ANXIETY

AN EMPOWERING GUIDE FOR YOUNG PEOPLE

WRITTEN BY
ANOUCHKA GROSE

ILLUSTRATED BY
LAURIANE BOHÉMIER

MAGIC CAT 🐱 PUBLISHING

NEW YORK

FOR ALL PEOPLE EVERYWHERE WHO ARE
WORKING TO PROTECT THE PLANET -A.G.

FOR ANYONE WHO WANTS TO CHANGE THE
WORLD, ONE ACT OF KINDNESS AT A TIME -L.B.

Although eco-anxiety is not currently a mental health diagnosis, it may impact some people more profoundly than others. If you find yourself struggling to cope, please reach out to a trusted adult, medical professional, or mental health resource.

The illustrations in this book were created digitally.
Set in Cherry, Wisely, and Wilden.

Library of Congress Control Number 2023936458
ISBN 978-1-4197-7136-1

Printed and bound in the United Arab Emirates
10 9 8 7 6 5 4 3 2 1

MIX
Paper | Supporting
responsible forestry
FSC® C004800

ABRAMS The Art of Books
195 Broadway, New York, NY 10007
abramsbooks.com

☮ Contents ☮

Welcome to this book about eco-anxiety.

I'm Anouchka, and I'm a psychoanalyst, which means I spend all day listening to people speak about their thoughts and feelings—especially the things that make them sad, angry, or scared. I work with young people, old people, and everyone in the middle. And, thanks to the internet, I work with people from all over the world. One of the things I hear more and more is that people are scared about the future of the planet. They say things like:

The last thing these people want to hear is, "Don't worry, it'll be fine." Sometimes their friends and family say this to them, and it makes them go, "Aaaaarrrggghh!" or even, "If everyone thought like that, we'd all be doomed!"

When people are worried about climate change, they need other people to take their fears seriously. In a sense, the more of us who are worried about it the better. But we also need to feel OK. We need to sleep, eat, and remember that life on Earth is an ongoing miracle. That's why we want to preserve it.

This book is a collection of all the things I've learned from working with people with eco-anxiety. It's a book that aims to care for the people most ready to help save the planet. I hope that reading it can help you to feel better. While I can't make the problem go away, I can tell you what scientists, activists, and people living in countries on the frontline of climate change have said about the things that have helped them. I can also tell you what helps me. There will be ten steps, and a tool kit at the end of each step that will give you ways to handle your thoughts and feelings.

The main thing you need to remember is that you're not alone. It's really important to talk about your fears and also to know that there are plenty of things you can do to help the planet.

In fact, if you have eco-anxiety, then congratulations! You're already halfway to being part of a solution . . .

What is eco-anxiety?

Eco-anxiety is extreme worry about current and future harm to the environment, and what I want you to understand about it is that it isn't a mental illness. **In fact, it's the exact opposite of an illness — it's a reasonable response to a real problem.** Some environmentalists aren't sure about the term "eco-anxiety" because it makes it sound like a clinical anxiety disorder — for example, social anxiety (fear of social situations) or separation anxiety (fear of losing the people you care about).

WHAT MAKES ECO-ANXIETY DIFFERENT IS THAT THE THING YOU'RE AFRAID OF IS ACTUALLY HAPPENING OUT THERE IN THE WORLD.

Because of this, some environmentalists prefer to use words like climate grief, eco-trauma, green guilt, or climate change distress. The advantage of these terms is that they don't make you sound like you're worrying unnecessarily. Plus, they make space for some of the other feelings you might be experiencing, like sadness, anger, shame, or even shutting down altogether.

Whatever term you prefer to use, if you're feeling any emotion right now, from anger to worry, I want you to know that you're far from alone. All of these feelings are absolutely normal, and we'll be exploring ways to manage them in the pages to come.

Who suffers from eco-anxiety?

Absolutely anyone and everyone! Young, old, rich, poor, city-dwellers, farmers, whoever. You could even argue that some people suffer from it without realizing. Maybe they're too busy working out how to feed their families to let themselves think about it. Or perhaps they're pretending it isn't happening. In any case, it's harder and harder not to notice that our planet is at risk, even if you try to push it to the back of your mind.

Eco-anxiety isn't a new thing, either. People have been speaking about it since the 1970s, when scientists and activists began warning people about the damage that was being done to the planet by fossil fuels, like coal and oil. Back then, climate change still seemed a long way off, and scientists and activists often felt like they weren't being listened to. To make it worse, some politicians and business owners wrote them off as a bunch of foolish "tree-huggers" (an epithet applied to someone who is very interested in protecting the environment). Now, with hindsight, we can probably agree that it was those politicians and business owners who were the foolish ones!

Today, more and more people are experiencing these feelings as we hear about the real effects of climate change in the news. You may see it on the television, on social media, or in magazines and newspapers. Some older people feel terrible for not having acted sooner, and younger people are often frightened about the future. **What is clear is that we're all in it together.**

Is eco-anxiety normal?

Yes, eco-anxiety is normal. However, not everyone's experience of eco-anxiety is the same. All of us are different, so we register the same ideas and events in different ways. Then there's the fact that climate change is more noticeable in very hot and very cold climates. While in the Global North people might be worried about the future, people in other parts of the world are already grappling with climate change. For example, people who live in Greenland and the Philippines are at opposite ends of the climate spectrum. Both countries are experiencing problems caused by extreme weather — either melting ice or storms.

CLIMATE CHANGE ISN'T JUST GOING ON "OVER THERE."
IT SHOWS US HOW WE'RE ALL CONNECTED.

The most important thing we can do is to look after ourselves, one another, and the planet. It's vital to remember to do all three. If we don't take care of ourselves, we won't be able to take care of anything else. **So, the first step toward starting to deal with your eco-anxiety is to remember that it's OK to give yourself a break.** Some people like to sit still and take a deep breath. Others like to escape into a book or film. Maybe you love to run around, dance, sing, draw, or make silly jokes. If it makes you feel better, do it!

≫≫ Step 1 ≪≪

Step Into
Your Feelings

WHEN YOU THINK ABOUT THE CLIMATE
CRISIS, HOW DOES IT MAKE YOU FEEL?

PANICKY? ANGRY? FRIGHTENED?
GUILTY? SAD?

You might feel some of these things at
different times, or even at the same
time. It might depend on something you
heard someone say, or something you
saw online. These emotions are horrible,
but you are not the only one feeling
this way.

Sometimes it can be hard to tell what a feeling even is.

Is it a thought? A sensation? Or something in between? Sometimes our feelings are triggered by events out in the world, and sometimes they suddenly explode from somewhere deep within us. One thing's for sure, they can be very hard to control. And eco-anxiety can be awful because it can feel like it will go on forever.

Mental signs of eco-anxiety include:

OUT-OF-CONTROL THOUGHTS

A SENSE OF DOOM

BRAIN FOG

GETTING CAUGHT UP IN THE FUTURE AND FORGETTING ABOUT THE PRESENT

Physical signs of eco-anxiety include:

FEELING SICK OR DIZZY

BREATHLESSNESS

A RACING HEART

HEADACHES

GOING CLAMMY ALL OVER

For most people, feelings of eco-anxiety come and go, only lasting a short time. This is because the human body isn't designed to exist in a constant state of emergency.

The other tricky thing about feelings is that it can be difficult to separate them all out. You might start by feeling sad, then angry, then you might feel guilty about your anger, and then anxious about how sad, angry, and guilty you feel. By the time someone asks you what's wrong, it's all such a mess in your head that you don't even know what to say, so you just say, "Hmph!" or sometimes you say nothing at all.

IT'S IMPORTANT TO REMEMBER THAT WHATEVER FEELINGS YOU'RE HAVING—EVEN IF THEY'RE NOT NICE TO FEEL—ARE OK.

The interesting part is knowing what to do next. It can sometimes feel as though feelings aren't allowed. As soon as you show that you are upset, people either try to cheer you up, or tell you to stop being silly. But feelings aren't silly at all—they are often very important.

Our feelings of eco-anxiety remind us that something is wrong. Some people deal with this by stamping their feelings out and refusing to acknowledge what's happening. Others might tell themselves it's all being solved—the politicians are working to fix it, and, if that fails, technology will rescue us. Ignoring our feelings can often feel like the best solution to stop the pain we feel. The relief we believe we'll feel by running away is very tempting. **But what if we listened to and engaged with our difficult feelings instead?**

In the same way that people from the same family or friendship group have very different ways of dealing with the same thing, everyone has their own ways of dealing with the climate crisis. Arguments can happen when people don't understand each other's ideas, feelings, and reactions. Sometimes it's helpful to remember that other people's coping mechanisms might be different from yours. If other people seem to be in denial, that's just their way of dealing with it. But it doesn't have to be yours. If you suffer from eco-anxiety, it's because your mind isn't letting you run away from the problem.

YOUR ECO-ANXIETY IS GIVING YOU A HINT. IT'S TELLING YOU TO JOIN IN THE EFFORT TO SAVE OUR PLANET.

It's important to know that your feelings about the climate crisis are legitimate. What's more, they have the potential to help you become part of the solution. Don't be hard on yourself. You should be proud of your feelings. They show that you are a well-informed, empathetic person who cares about the state of the world. We don't want to get rid of your eco-anxiety, but to help you think of it instead as eco-compassion, eco-understanding, eco-action, and eco-determination. It's a small switch from eco-worrier to eco-warrior—but you have to be worried in the first place to make it!

WE CAN'T TAKE
ACTION TO PROTECT
OUR PLANET IF WE
ARE IN DENIAL THAT
THERE IS A PROBLEM
TO BEGIN WITH

Self-care practices to ease your eco-anxiety

FOCUS ON THINGS THAT BRING YOU JOY

It might be true to say that eco-anxiety is helpful for triggering action. It's also true that a love of life is a great motivator when it comes to preserving our world. Making time for things you love will make you a more effective eco-ally.

TALK TO SOMEONE YOU TRUST

It's awful to deal with bad feelings alone. Speak to someone you feel comfortable with and who will give you time to express your thoughts.

BE KIND TO YOURSELF

Nobody's perfect, and the fact that you're worried at all shows you are at the beginning of your journey toward becoming the best eco-ally you can be.

LEARN MORE ABOUT CLIMATE CHANGE

Learn about the things you can do to make a difference, however big or small. We can often alleviate a fear of the unknown by educating ourselves about the situation in question.

LISTEN TO YOUR BODY

Next time you watch the news and feel your heart speed up or your palms sweating, check in with yourself and say, "Thank you, body, for reminding me how precious the world is. Please trust that I am doing what I can for now."

How to accept and value your feelings

1   VALIDATE YOUR ECO-ANXIETY

Whenever you feel eco-anxiety kick in, remind yourself that's it's a perfectly rational response to a real problem. Your eco-anxiety is a sign that your ideas and emotions are in tune.

2   REJECT DENIAL

Once you've acknowledged that there's a problem, the only way is forward. Denial might seem to work well for some people, but for those of us with eco-anxiety, it isn't really an option ... and that's OK!

3   USE YOUR FEELINGS TO SPARK ACTION

Validating your feelings is the first step, and taking action is the second. Without action, all the validation in the world could seem a little empty.

4   FOSTER DETERMINATION

If you set yourself a realistic goal, like "to live as responsibly and sustainably as possible," then you will increase your chances of achieving it. Forgive the odd slip up. It's not possible to be eco-perfect!

5   BE TOLERANT OF OTHERS

Belittling someone for having a different opinion from yours won't convince them to change their mind, but a thoughtful discussion might.

Challenge the Voice in Your Head

WE'VE ALL GOT A VOICE IN OUR HEAD. WHAT DOES YOURS SAY?

MINE SOMETIMES SAYS, "WHAT'S THE POINT IN EVEN TRYING?"

The voice you hear inside your head is called inner speech. Inner speech allows us to narrate our own lives, as though we're having a conversation with ourselves. This is healthy, but sometimes this inner speech can say something negative and become an inner critic. When this happens, we must empower ourselves to challenge it.

Whose voice is it anyway?

The strange thing about the voices in our heads is that it can be hard to say exactly whether they come from inside us or outside us. On the one hand, you could say they are our thoughts and no one else's. But who taught us how to think? The world bombards us with ideas and opinions, and we gravitate toward some and steer clear of others. Still, our ideas and opinions can change. If the people around us don't seem bothered about climate change, it can be easy to treat some of their opinions as if they were our own. Sometimes we can even find ourselves having a private argument in our own head! Maybe it goes something like this:

> POSITIVE YOU: We need to make sustainable changes to the way we live if we want to have a future.

> NEGATIVE YOU: But will it make a difference if only a few of us bother?

> POSITIVE YOU: Well, if some of us show that it can be done, it might influence others to act.

> NEGATIVE YOU: I doubt it. You can't even influence your teacher to give you less homework!

Psychologists call these voices cognitive dissonance. Cognitive dissonance means having two or more opposing ideas at the same time. Maybe you think it's pointless to eat a plant-based diet because hardly anyone else that you know does. But you also feel terrible every time you eat a beef burger. Or you've been told that recycling isn't going to save the world, but you can't bear to see a garbage can full of old food, paper, plastic, and metal all mixed together.

One irritating feature of these conflicting voices is that it can be hard to tell which one's the real you. Do you sincerely care about the planet but have a tendency to undermine your good intentions with self-destructive thoughts? Or is the real truth that you don't really want to have to go to a lot of effort to change your lifestyle as the effects of climate change don't impact you every day? For many of us, it tends to be a bit of both. We really do want what's best for the world, but we also know that we can sometimes be selfish or careless.

A certain amount of cognitive dissonance is inevitable—only a robot could be programmed to have perfectly consistent ideas! The rest of us have to accept a bit of psychological confusion. In fact, it's a sign that we are capable of complex thinking—it's good to be able to see both sides of an argument.

STILL, WHEN IT COMES TO TAKING CLIMATE ACTION, IT'S HELPFUL TO MAKE A CLEAR DECISION ABOUT WHICH VOICES TO LISTEN TO.

You may not remember this, but in 2019, Greta Thunberg told an American Congressional Hearing, "I don't want you to listen to me. I want you to listen to the scientists." This is a helpful way of thinking about who to listen to when we think about the climate crisis. There's no denying that scientists enjoy a good argument, but when it comes to climate change there is no debate. Scientists across the board agree that we need to act to reduce our carbon footprint—the total amount of greenhouse gases (including carbon dioxide and methane) that are generated by our actions. Every step we take in this direction is worthwhile. So, if a voice in your head is telling you it's all pointless, you should tell that voice to be quiet.

IN THE BATTLE BETWEEN SCIENTIFIC EVIDENCE AND YOUR PESKY INNER CRITIC, LET THE SCIENTISTS WIN!

Instead, remind the voice that it's science that has helped us to understand the problem and offers us the methods to solve it. Science drives action, and Greta Thunberg once famously said, "No one is too small to make a difference." I think we all should definitely listen to that! This doesn't mean we have to get super-stressed thinking of every possible thing we can do. It just means we should do something. If all of us make little differences today, it will make a massive difference to tomorrow.

A POSITIVE
MINDSET BRINGS
POSITIVE ACTION

How to talk nicely to your inner critic

If you find yourself overthinking, or getting into private arguments, don't worry. It's just a sign that your brain is taking all sorts of information into account. But instead of getting into an argument with your inner critic, you could try having a polite word. Here's an example:

POSITIVE YOU: Let's turn the thermostat down by one degree.

NEGATIVE YOU: What will that do to help anything?

POSITIVE YOU: It's just one small change among many. I will also stop eating meat for the entire month of January.

NEGATIVE YOU: The holidays followed by a month of lentils. Ugh!

POSITIVE YOU: You liked those veggie sausages. And tomato sauce is vegan!

NEGATIVE YOU: If you say so.

POSITIVE YOU: I do, and what I say is important. You should listen to me, too.

Ways to ease your inner critic

REMIND YOURSELF YOU'RE NOT A ROBOT

Being human is very complicated, and we can't always control the thoughts that run through our heads. You can only try your best.

ASK QUESTIONS

Ask where that negative thought came from. Is it like something you heard on the radio? Just because you thought it, it doesn't mean you have to keep thinking it. Perhaps it belongs to someone else anyhow.

RESPECT YOUR NEGATIVE VOICES

Negative voices are proof that your brain is hard at work. Don't feel bad about your own selfish, angry, or defeatist thoughts — your mind is just sifting through the evidence. Confusion is very often a sign of intelligence.

LET SCIENCE GIVE YOU HOPE

The evidence tells us that the climate scientists are right, and the scientists are telling us not to give up hope. The science is very clear — there are still lots of things we can do. So let's do them!

BE KIND TO YOUR NEGATIVE SELF

Just because your inner voices don't always agree, you don't need to become a human battlefield. If you become good at talking them down nicely, you will soon be ready to persuade real-life climate defeatists to start being more sensible!

Find Your Path to Action

BY TRANSFORMING YOUR ECO-ANXIETY
INTO HEARTFELT PURPOSE, YOU WILL
BE LAUNCHED INTO ACTION.

BUT WHICH ACTIONS ARE RIGHT FOR YOU?

Some people seem to know what they want to do, while for others it can take a little time. False starts are all part of the process. The important thing is to keep going! Every step toward making a better world is worth taking, even if you trip up along the way.

Your eco-anxiety can help you to find your purpose.

We've already said a bit about treating your eco-anxiety as a friend, but it's time to delve a little deeper. Not only can it be a friend, but also a life coach and trusted advisor. Your eco-anxiety is prodding you to take climate action. The reason it feels stressful is because it means business. It won't stop until it feels listened to. This is the science of eco-anxiety. You perceive a threat and your body wants to save you from that threat, so it does all sorts of things that it thinks will help. It's hard to ignore eco-anxiety because it feels so unpleasant. That's part of its genius. It releases stress hormones into your system, which cause your heart to speed up, your blood pressure to increase, your pupils to widen, all of which causes your brain to think faster and your muscles to tighten.

This whole bodily chain reaction is triggered by the sympathetic nervous system. When you're feeling panicky, that might not sound like the most appropriate name for it. But if you take a minute to think about it, your body is really trying to help you. In prehistoric times, that might have involved propelling you to run away from a bear. These days it may also involve propelling you to ask your parents to run the washing machine with cold water. The one thing it won't let you do is nothing. If it sees you doing nothing it will bug you until you do something.

You may be asking, but what exactly is the right thing to do? Before we answer that question, we might need to know about the parasympathetic nervous system. This is our body's natural antidote to the stress reactions we've just described. For example, once it's been established that you've successfully run away from a bear, your body sends out a new batch of signals telling your heart to slow down and your breathing to return to normal. Of course, this doesn't mean that your body will only give you a break once the climate crisis is fixed. Our bodies are a bit more practical than that. It's exhausting to stay in emergency mode all the time, so if your body gets the message that something is being done, it will gladly take the hint. You can even slow down your breathing on purpose to tell the system to kick in. **Aren't our bodies amazing!**

THIS IS WHAT PEOPLE MEAN WHEN THEY SAY, "THE CURE FOR ECO-ANXIETY IS ECO-ACTION"—IT'S ACTUALLY A BIOLOGICALLY SOUND THEORY.

The good news is that climate action takes many, many forms. "Action" covers everything from short-term to long-term, small acts to big acts. Anything from not eating meat on a Monday to going plastic-free, to committing to making your global corporation carbon-neutral counts. Sometimes people say, "But I can't do everything!" This is true. The point is to find a realistic position on the scale between doing nothing and doing everything.

In a sense, the first and most important thing you need to do is to acknowledge that there is a real problem. This is horrible, but it's also a genuine act of bravery. If you're reading this book, it's probably because you've already done the hard part. Go you! Once your brain and body are in agreement that something needs to be done, it becomes easier and easier to do it... and harder and harder not to do it!

I'm guessing you've already done this part too, but for a lot of people, the next step is to look for ideas for things you can do. Eating less meat is a great idea, as people who eat a vegetarian diet tend to have a far lower carbon footprint than those who are meat- or fish-eaters. Rewilding your garden is also a brilliant idea (or someone else's providing they give their permission, of course!), as you could reintroduce native plants that might have lived in the garden previously but do not anymore. There are hundreds, if not thousands, of these things out there — so I'm not going to fill up the rest of this book by writing a list! Any or all of them are worth doing. You can look them up and take your pick. Just remember: All climate action is worthwhile.

Lastly, when people belittle the concerns of environmentalists, it's because they haven't understood the situation. Once you've seen the scale of the problem, it stops being a pain to make small sacrifices, or to do things that require a little bravery. If there are things you can do, go for it! As you get older there will be more and more things you can do. And make sure you bring others on the journey with you — I'm sure you could teach some adults a great deal!

How to transform your eco-anxiety into action

THINK OF ECO-ANXIETY AS A FRIEND

Your eco-anxiety is trying to make the world a safer place for you. I like to think of mine as a friend who can be annoying but means well.

REALIZE YOU DON'T HAVE TO FIX THE PROBLEM ALL AT ONCE

Start by making little changes in your personal life. And don't let people tell you there's no point. If more of us make small differences, it will add up to big changes.

REMEMBER THAT YOU ARE NOT ALONE

A study from 2021 found that 75 percent of young people said the planet's future felt frightening. That's a real majority, and there's power to be found in the collective.

DO THE THINGS YOU CAN AND WORRY LESS ABOUT THE THINGS YOU CAN'T

It's possible to take the emergency seriously and still love life. Some people say they feel bad if they stop feeling bad. I know what they mean, but try not to let that be you!

TAKE A FEW DEEP BREATHS

Even if your parasympathetic nervous system is slow to get the message, you can tell yourself that there are few actions less harmful to the planet than simply breathing.

How to find your path

FIND YOUR PEOPLE

Activism doesn't have to involve a protest. It might include taking a nature-appreciation walk or joining a group that gets together to talk and support one another. You can try a few different activities and see what suits you.

INVOLVE OTHER PEOPLE

Perhaps you could get your school to celebrate Earth Day, or convince your family to join a neighborhood cleanup. All of these things can be fun and are great for raising awareness.

EDUCATE YOURSELF

Food is a good place to start. Not all environmentally aware people are vegan There are plenty of good arguments for responsible flexitarianism.

JOIN A CLUB

Joining a environmental club can not only help to make you feel part of a community. It can also give you new and exciting ideas for ways that young people can combat climate change.

MAKE LONG-TERM ECO-PLANS

Maybe you will be a green town planner or even a world leader. If people tell you there's no point in giving up eating fish, you can tell them it's just an interim plan while you work on preventing people from overfishing!

Find the Right Balance of Information

THE INFORMATION WE CONSUME TRULY MATTERS.

WE NEED TO KNOW THE TRUTH, BUT WE ALSO NEED TO HAVE HOPE.

Relying on inaccurate information or having a lack of knowledge can make it hard to understand abstract problems like climate change. It's important to focus on the facts, but also to balance real worries with up-to-date news about all the incredible work people are doing to respond to the problem.

How do we know what's true?

It's all very well to say, "Follow the science," and "Listen to the facts." But how do we know who's telling the truth? To start, not all scientists agree with each other. Different scientists might care about one aspect of climate change more than another, and as a result they might disagree about which theory is better. After all, there are many types of climate scientists working across different fields — such as meteorology (the study of Earth's atmosphere and weather), biochemistry (the chemistry of living organisms), and geophysics (Earth's physical processes) — and scientists in different fields have different ideas about how we should be responding to climate change. Should we focus on global food systems, fuel use, or manufacturing? Or is it only any use if we think of all three at once? We might believe our current political and economic systems are not doing enough and say, "We want system change, not climate change." But scientists don't all agree on which new systems would be most effective.

THE ONE THING SCIENTISTS AGREE ON ALMOST UNANIMOUSLY IS THAT CLIMATE CHANGE IS CAUSED BY HUMANS.

In 2021, research involving 90,000 climate-related studies found that 99.9 percent of scientists agreed that anthropogenic (human-related) climate change is real. The lead author on the study came out and said, "It is really case closed. There is nobody of significance in the scientific community who doubts human-caused climate change." The reason they used the phrase "case closed" is because the rapid rise of social media in the last decade brought with it a surge in climate misinformation from people whose business it was to make science look like opinion. These people are known as climate change deniers. Thankfully, as time goes on, climate change deniers are being called out and it's becoming more and more difficult to spread lies about climate change. Even the most reputable news outlets may be frustratingly uninterested in climate change, but at least the stories that appear there should be properly fact-checked. Social media, however, isn't regulated in this way and is still pretty much the Wild West where climate information is concerned.

If you've picked up this book, I know you'll agree it's important to listen to the scientists, not people on social media. But I want to tell you that it's fine to not listen to them all the time! Sometimes we might rather listen to music, or the birdsong outside. The newspaper I read, for example, aims to report consistently and responsibly about climate change. This means there are numerous upsetting articles every day that sometimes make me feel sick with worry. I regularly skip that section if I'm not in the mood to digest it there and then. **Remember, if there's an important new piece of information, it will always reach you somehow — it won't just disappear from the news after one day.**

Once you're engaged with the climate crisis, you don't need to absorb every new bit of proof that the world is at risk. This is not going to make you a better environmentalist, it's just going to make you very unhappy. So be kind to yourself and tell yourself it's OK to switch off the news and open your eyes and ears to other things. It's all about balance.

Plus, on the bright side, people all over the world are working really hard to slow down climate change. There are scientists, activists, politicians, Indigenous Elders, business people, young people, plants, insects, all doing everything in their power to sustain a healthy planet. We need to hear their stories, too. Cristiana Figueres, who was instrumental in bringing about the Paris Climate Agreement (which aims to keep the world below 1.5 degrees of warming), has coined the term "stubborn optimism" to describe a constructive attitude toward the future of the environment. **We mustn't give in to pessimism, as this might stop us fighting to make important changes.** But you have to be stubborn to be an optimist when there's so much bad news around!

Not only will good news make you feel better, it will help you to cultivate the kind of mental attitude most likely to make a positive difference to the world. One easy way to get a dose of optimism is simply to tap the words "good climate news" into a search engine. I just did this and learned that in the future, airplanes might be designed to run on sugar-eating bacteria, that surgeons are developing climate-friendly operations, and that dolphin excrement may hold the key to saving coral reefs!

REMEMBER THAT
READING GOOD NEWS IS
JUST AS IMPORTANT AS
READING BAD NEWS

Climate change resources

WWW.CLIMATEKIDS.NASA.GOV

NASA Climate Kids is produced by scientists at NASA and explains climate change and provides simple explanations of complex problems.

WWW.DOGONEWS.COM

Dogo News is a bilingual kids' news website that you can read in English or Spanish. It has an environment section, as well as science, social studies, world news, and what they call "civics," which means stories about people.

WWW.KIDS.NATIONALGEOGRAPHIC.COM

National Geographic Kids is a magazine with a focus on the natural world. They also have a fantastic website with information about climate change and tips for making a difference.

WWW.KIDSNEWS.COM.AU

Kids News is a Australian news website where you can choose articles that match your reading level. It's important to listen to what the Australians have to say about the environment as, like many countries, it is on the front line of climate change.

WWW.TIMEFORKIDS.COM

Time magazine devotes a section of their website to news tailored especially to children. They cover all sorts of news, not just environmental, so you can also read international science, history, and community news stories.

How to fuel your stubborn optimism

TRUST THE 99.9 PERCENT OF SCIENTISTS

Not only are they in agreement about the reality of the climate emergency, but many of them are busy working on solutions.

STAY INFORMED

Rather than being drowned by the daily drip of news, just stay informed about the big picture. The Intergovernmental Panel on Climate Change (IPCC) issues a report on climate change every few years, and you can read summaries online.

ALLOW YOURSELF TO SWITCH OFF

A study from 2013 found that watching the news can decrease your creativity—and what this planet needs is creative people, so learn to switch it off!

REJECT THE TERM "DOOMER"

This is a word that can be used to shut down anyone who's concerned about the impact of climate change. If anyone calls you a doomer, refer them to the IPCC report and ask them if they think they know better than the scientists!

SEEK OUT POSITIVE STORIES

Instead of scrolling mindlessly on your phone, take control of the information you consume. Search for something nice! This will fuel your determination for tomorrow.

Reclaim Your Power

THE CLIMATE CRISIS CAN MAKE US FEEL CONFUSED AND POWERLESS.

BUT IF WE CHANGE THE WAY WE THINK, WE CAN GET OUR POWER BACK!

Thinking about the scale of climate change can make us feel helpless as individuals—and individual action may seem like a drop in the ocean in comparison to big businesses. I want you to discard the belief that you're powerless: You're incredibly powerful.

It's time to clear up climate confusion.

Putting the climate deniers aside, even environmentalists can give mixed messaging about what we should be doing to avert the climate crisis. Some people say the best thing we can do is to stop flying, others say to switch to a plant-based diet. But then again, you will hear some people say that individual action is pointless if massive change doesn't happen at a societal level. So, who's right? Maybe it's helpful to understand a little bit more about why some environmentalists are less keen on the idea of individual action. It's certainly not because they think eating less meat and using less fossil fuel are bad ideas. They are just questioning the notion that each of us should be taking full responsibility for the climate in our private lives while some governments and big businesses don't play their part.

WE MUST SHARE RESPONSIBILITY FOR THE STATE OF THE PLANET.

If we all feel like we're privately responsible, then it can make the problem seem insoluble, which leads to despair and guilt, because we can never do enough. This not only makes us feel awful, it allows those big organizations to carry on making money while polluting our world. How unfair is that?

Instead of trying to solve the problem of whether we should be cutting out meat or canceling our summer travel, we would be better off saying we can do either or both. It's all worthwhile. This doesn't mean we have to be performing all manner of environmental action at all times! This is another one of those unhelpful thought patterns that just makes us feel bad. It's much more productive to think that we'll do what we can when we can. And, if we act together, we can do a lot.

While environmentalists who say we ought to be focusing all our energy on massive societal change surely mean well, their message risks playing into the hands of the very people they are hoping to challenge. If we all stopped recycling and started eating beef for every meal, would that give us any more time or resources to lobby for change? No! But would it give governments and big businesses an excuse to say, "Why should we care about the planet when no one else seems to?"

 OUR SMALL ACTS CAN SHOW PEOPLE IN POWER THAT WE MEAN BUSINESS.

There are many more of us than there are of them. **If we all act according to our principles, it forces the powerful people to listen to us.** If our governments do things we disapprove of, we won't vote for them. If businesses do things we disappove of, we won't buy their products. So, who's got the power now?

The idea that we have to choose between the personal and the political is wrong. I think it's much more sensible to follow the feminists of the 1960s, who said, "The personal is political." What we do in our private lives matters on the grand scale: There's a real strength in numbers. If we all agree we'd like a habitable planet, then we can bring about monumental change by living in sustainable ways and creating virtuous circles where our own actions lend support and impetus to the actions of others. Social scientists agree that our individual actions on climate have significant effects on the behavior of the people around us.

THE MATH IS SIMPLE—THE MORE OF US WHO WORK TO KEEP EARTH HEALTHY, THE MORE WE SHOW OTHER PEOPLE THAT THERE IS A POINT IN TRYING. IT ALL ADDS UP!

We hear a lot about negative tipping points—moments beyond which icebergs can't stay frozen, or insect species can't reproduce. But we need to start working toward positive tipping points, where entire populations stop buying from polluting businesses and withdraw support from leaders who fail to protect our precious ecosystems. If we keep pushing in the right direction, we can make ourselves part of a powerful mass. Huge numbers of people doing small things can be more powerful than a few people doing big things. And all sorts of people doing all manner of environmentally responsible things, big and small, is the very best option of all.

Eco-friendly activities

Given that none of us is likely to be elected president anytime soon, we have to learn to make the best use of the powers we have. Get a notepad and pen and make a list of some things you can do to help slow down climate change.

HERE ARE SOME IDEAS:

 Walk rather than taking the car whenever possible

 Plant wildflowers to help butterflies and bees

 Avoid single-use, disposable items

Switch off appliances when you're not using them

Save energy and water by being quick in the shower

That's a great start already. Now, take your list and see how you could turbo-charge it. First of all, ask yourself which groups you are a part of. This can be anything from your family to your team or club. Are there ways you can involve other people?

 Could you get everyone on your street to turn off their home electronic devices when they aren't using them?

 Could you take control of the school garden to make it a refuge for insects?

 Could you get your entire soccer team to use reusable water bottles?

How to cultivate your power

RAISE AWARENESS

If you make a list of actions and bring other people on board, not only will there be more people doing those actions, you will be showing them how it's possible to make a difference.

TRY TO MAKE IT FUN

One myth about environmentalists is that we're gloomy people, when actually we love the planet and want to preserve fun for eternity! When you're trying to involve other people, do what you can to make sure they have a good time.

Level up!

BE AMBITIOUS

Treat getting people on board like a video game with ascending levels. For example, if you get your parents to agree to switch to an ethical bank account, maybe you could then suggest that the companies they work for do the same.

DON'T BE PUT OFF BY FAILURE

It's not always easy to do this stuff. Sometimes you have to have ten ideas in order to make just one of them a reality. Having positive hopes can fuel your motivation to persevere.

FIND YOUR POWER—AND (OAT) MILK IT!

Perhaps your special power will be to use your youthful exuberance to make older people listen. Youth is the not-so-secret weapon of the environmental movement. Use it before you grow up!

Take Action Where You Can

DID YOU KNOW THAT HUMAN BRAINS AREN'T BUILT TO RESPOND EASILY TO LARGE, SLOW-MOVING THREATS?

OUR BRAINS ACTUALLY RESIST ACTION.

When something feels too big to deal with, like climate change, our brains will often switch off or focus on something that is easier. So be kind to yourself and others if you feel not enough is being done. With a thoughtful approach, you will be able to stay on track and bring other people along with you.

Not all minds think alike.

Most human brains are excellent at reacting to fast-moving threats. For example, if a ball is flying straight toward your head, you might find yourself jumping out of the way before you've had even a second to think about it. Slow threats, however, are much better at getting around our built-in alarm systems. This is because we're always processing such huge amounts of information that we tend to focus on the things that require our immediate attention. However, some of us seem to be more inclined to react to slow threats than others. **People with eco-anxiety are more willing and more able to consider distant hazards.**

The human brain generally is much more able to deal with certainty than uncertainty, because responding to uncertainty often requires more complex calculations. Although we are now certain that climate change is real, we can't predict exactly how and when it will unfold. The human brain is constantly weeding out information in order to avoid brain overload. If it tried to plan for absolutely everything, it would soon go into meltdown! **However, people with eco-anxiety are more ready to allow for uncertainty without trying to shut it down.** The downside of this is that, having understood the scale of the climate emergency, it can become **ALL** we can think about. It's as if the only possible reactions are indifference or panic, and this isn't good for our mind or body. Luckily for our mental health, this isn't the case. We can focus on some more positive features of our incredible human brains. Not only can they react quickly in order to save us from immediate threats, but they are also good at working out difficult problems and imagining various futures.

WE CAN APPEAL TO THE HUMAN BRAIN
WHEN IT COMES TO CLIMATE CHANGE.

We are able to understand why it's happening, and we are also perfectly capable of understanding what we need to do to stop it. For example, we know we need to give up overconsuming harmful oil and gas and switch to cleaner, renewable energy sources. And we know this because the brains of brilliant scientists have consistently come to this conclusion.

Of course, that makes it sound a bit too easy! In order to do that, millions of people would have to get on board. The good news is that even the most resistant people finally seem to be grasping the idea that something needs to be done. If the climate crisis is like a ball traveling toward our heads in extreme slow motion, it's close enough now that even the slow-reactors are realizing it's going to hurt if we don't do something, and soon. Perhaps we could say that this historical moment has something in common with a forest fire. It will just take a few bright sparks to ignite humanity's passion to get on with the job. And maybe one of those sparks is you!

If the best hope we have of making a difference is to galvanize as many people as possible into action, then we must be clever about how we present the problem. Even if our unhelpful inner critic is telling us, "It's a total disaster! Everyone's useless! It's too late!" we have to tell it to give us a minute while we think of a more inspiring message.

The good thing about the human brain is that it's always trying to work out what's best for us. Sometimes it miscalculates and chooses things that are good in the short-term but bad in the long-term—like eating sweets instead of vegetables! If you tell people that the world will soon be destroyed, they might very well decide to have a party on the way out. But if you explain to them that we can actually make a big difference in a short time, then they will be far more likely to respond constructively. The vast majority of people really do agree that the best thing for all of us is to take care of the only world we've got. It's pretty much a no-brainer.

I'd like you to visualize yourself as a tiny spark of pure energy. Tell yourself you're going to use this energy to fire up everyone you meet. When people see the passion you put into making a better world, they'll join forces, and together you'll burn even brighter. We know how to save our wonderful planet—so let's get on with it!

Learn something new

Give your brain a treat. These documentaries are packed full of ideas, knowledge, and inspiration to help you turn your thoughts into actions:

1 2040

A documentary about what we could achieve using existing ideas and technology to counteract climate change. Made by a father who gives us a hopeful vision of what it's possible to achieve by the time his children grow up.

2 BEFORE THE FLOOD

Film star Leonardo DiCaprio takes us on a journey to learn about the climate emergency. We meet scientists who teach us the science behind climate change, and we also hear the possible solutions.

3 I AM GRETA

A close-up portrait of the globally famous teenage climate activist, Greta Thunberg.

4 LIVING ON ONE DOLLAR

A group of friends goes to rural Guatemala to find out what it's like to live on a dollar a day, as 1.1 billion people on the planet currently do.

5 OUR PLANET

Narrated by David Attenborough, this eight-part series looks at the ways in which human activities are affecting wildlife all over the world.

Set up a climate action group

GET AT LEAST ONE TEACHER INVOLVED

They will be able to help you with practicalities like where to have meetings. You will also need the school's permission to set up the group.

SPREAD THE WORD

Put up flyers or put a notice in the school newsletter to let everyone know you're setting up a climate action group. Give notice so that everyone who wants to be there can make it.

MAKE A PLAN FOR YOUR FIRST MEETING

It's important that the people who come feel that there is a point in being there. Suggest some activities that you could all do together—write letters, organize petitions, and so on.

KEEP MOMENTUM GOING

End each meeting with a good plan for the next one. Some groups fizzle out if it feels like no one knows what they're doing. Always aim to give people a reason to come back. Having lots of activities will make it fun as well as purposeful.

USE SOCIAL MEDIA

With the help of an adult, make a video to share on social media. Anything to get your message out there. Who knows, you might even end up as a positive climate story on the evening news!

⇝⇝ Step 7 ⇜⇜

Find Comfort in Community

FINDING PEOPLE WHO FEEL SIMILAR TO YOU CAN BE A HUGE HELP WHEN EXPERIENCING ECO-ANXIETY.

WE ALL NEED SUPPORT AT SOME POINT, AND WE CAN ALSO SUPPORT OTHERS.

There's no need to struggle alone with eco-anxiety, especially not when so many of us are feeling the same. Working with other people who also want to protect the environment can bring a sense of connection. Moving toward solutions together can give us a much greater feeling of hope in overwhelming circumstances.

A safe space is a place where you feel safe to be honest.

I've shared a lot in this book about staying optimistic and sending out positive messages, but what about the times when we feel really sad, angry, and hopeless? These are real feelings, with real causes, so they need a real outlet. It's no good keeping our faces frozen into smiles while we're feeling horrible inside.

THE GREAT THING ABOUT TALKING ABOUT YOUR ENVIRONMENTAL WORRIES WITH OTHER PEOPLE WHO FEEL THE SAME IS THAT THEY WON'T JUDGE YOU, AND THEY WON'T TRY TO TALK YOU OUT OF IT.

There is an eco-philosopher called Timothy Morton who coined the phrase "the ecological thought." It means the moment when you realize that all is not well with the environment on a truly momentous, complex scale. "Thought" doesn't even quite feel like the right word for it—it's just so huge. Once you've had this thought, it would be very, very difficult to unthink it. You can't go backward, so you just have to keep going forward.

People who have had the ecological thought are well-equipped to be kind to one another. We all know what it's like to feel the panic and grief that comes with understanding the damage that's being done to our world. If we know that someone else is feeling this way too, our hearts immediately go out to them.

There are many reasons to open up and share feelings. If people don't know how you feel, they won't be able to help you, which is not only bad for you, it's bad for them, too. It's terrible when you can see that someone feels sad but you have no idea why. If people know you're having a hard time, they can validate your feelings, and they might also help you to see things slightly differently. There's also the unfortunate fact that bad feelings have a habit of hanging around until you acknowledge them. Ignoring them doesn't necessarily make them go away. You'll be amazed to see how helpful it is to share your feelings with someone else who's had the ecological thought.

 IN ORDER TO STRIVE FOR A BETTER WORLD, IT HELPS TO BELIEVE IN THE GOODNESS OF OTHERS.

When you share your difficult feelings with other people, you are giving them a chance to take care of you. You don't need to feel that you are asking a favor or adding a burden. Not only will you feel less alone, but so will the people you're sharing with. It's lovely to be there for one another, and one day you will be able to take care of someone else who's suffering.

Building communities of like-minded people is helpful for increasing momentum and showing it's possible to act positively. But what about the people who don't seem so bothered? It can be easy to get frustrated with them and blame them for all the world's problems, but it isn't really their fault. Also, if we want them to join us in our fight against climate change, it's important that we don't start too many arguments with them!

We need to find a balance between seeking out people we can share our feelings with honestly and keeping a place open for people who don't feel the same way, or who are just a few steps behind. The ecological thought is very uncomfortable in the beginning, and perhaps not everyone is ready to have it. But once you've had it you can start to learn to live with it, and even to find a certain peace in the idea that at least now you know you can do something about it.

By being there with and for other people who are ready and willing to take care of the planet, we can demonstrate to everyone that it's OK to acknowledge the uncomfortable truth. We have to go through a painful period of mental adjustment, but in the end it's better than trying to pretend it isn't happening. It's always inspiring to meet other people who have let themselves confront the agonizing realities of climate change but are still capable of happiness, kindness, and optimism.

SURROUND YOURSELF WITH PEOPLE WHO INSPIRE YOU

Climate Café

Have you heard of Climate Cafés? They happen all around the world, and they show people they are not alone in their fears.

WHAT IS A CLIMATE CÁFE?

A Climate Café is a place where anyone can come to discuss thoughts and feelings about the climate emergency.

CAN ANYONE GO?

Many Climate Cafés are for people who are over 18, so you'd need to look for one that welcomes younger people. Be sure to discuss with an adult before you attend.

WHERE CAN I FIND ONE?

You could look online for "Climate Cafés near me." Alternatively, you could ask an adult to help you plan one for people in your school or community. Visit **www.climateandmind.org/climate-cafe** for tips.

WHAT'S THE POINT IN JUST TALKING?

If we sense we are alone with our feelings on climate change, not only will we suffer them more, but we will feel powerless to act. But after having had a good chat at a Climate Café, we might then feel empowered to act!

WHAT IF I'M TOO SHY?

It can be hard to talk about upsetting ideas in front of a group of people, but Climate Cafés are safe spaces, and people find them inspiring, positive places to attend.

How to be a good listener

When we feel upset, we often turn to others for help and support. So when others come to us, we should do our best to help them feel better.

1 GIVE THE OTHER PERSON TIME

Sometimes it's difficult to find the right words for things. It can even take a few tries. Be patient and give the other person your time.

2 SHOW INTEREST

There's nothing worse than speaking to someone who looks bored. You can show interest through your body language, like looking the person who's speaking in the eye.

3 ASK QUESTIONS

This is not only a great way to express interest, but it can help the other person to think in new ways. We can sometimes surprise ourselves with what we learn, too!

4 DON'T TRY TO SOLVE EVERYTHING

When people are upset it can be tempting to rush in with solutions. It's enough that you're being kind and listening, you don't have to fix everything as well!

5 LISTEN WITHOUT JUDGING

Try to focus on listening, rather than reacting. If you start reacting emotionally to what's being said, then it can get in the way of listening to what is said next.

Build Your Resilience

RESILIENCE IS THE ABILITY TO COPE WHEN THINGS GO WRONG.

WHEN YOU FEEL OVERWHELMED BY THE CLIMATE CRISIS, THERE ARE MENTAL HABITS THAT CAN HELP YOU TO BOUNCE BACK.

Your resilience is affected by a number of factors, including your age. But you can learn to become more resilient. Resilience is like a muscle—it can take a while to build it up, but it's worth the effort because eventually you become much stronger.

How can I build up my resilience?

We can learn resilience from wind-resistant plants. Some plants, like palms and conifers, are very good at growing in windy places. They tend to have bendy stems and narrow leaves so they can flex and sway without getting knocked over. So, just like palms and conifers, rather than staying stiff and still, we can cultivate supple ways of thinking and adapting to new situations.

WHEN THE WINDS OF CHANGE BLOW, WE NEED TO SWAY WITH THEM!

In order to become more resilient, we have to learn to cope better with uncertainty. As we've already seen in Step 6, this is sometimes easier said than done. Still, anyone who remembers living through the COVID-19 pandemic knows that the whole world can change in the space of a few weeks, and that it's possible to find ways to move with it. Although the COVID-19 pandemic was extremely hard for many, many people, it also showed that we can find ingenious ways to survive extraordinary events. While millions of us were shut in our houses for months on end, we still often found things to do. Maybe we grew our own food or wrote letters to our friends. Perhaps some of us even came out of it a little wiser! One of the greatest forms of resilience is to be able to find happiness in unusual circumstances — and the pandemic certainly provided lots of opportunities to practice just that.

Situations like the COVID-19 pandemic teach us that the world operates independently of our wills and wishes. We might want one thing and get another. The thing about living in an industrialized society is that we are led to expect so many aspects of our lives to remain stable and under our control. Our houses keep us warm in winter and cool in summer. Fresh fruits and vegetables are available year-round. Not only that, but our economic systems are designed to give us the impression that everything is running smoothly, even when it isn't. It's hardly surprising that so many of us are so terrified of change. But this is not a healthy way to live.

Although we don't know exactly how and when climate change will begin to seriously affect us, we can be fairly sure it will. And of course, if we are involved in the fight to slow it down, that would suggest we see the changes as undesirable. Still, this doesn't mean the future will be horrible. It will be different, for sure, but different isn't always bad. I'm certainly not saying, "Climate change doesn't matter because we will adapt." **It's more that given we know it's happening, we need to trust we will apply our ingenuity to the new challenges we face.** In a sense, life is resilience. Plants grow, wounds heal, species adapt. Life bends to new circumstances. This is what we mean when we say "life force." Life itself seems to want to keep going.

For younger people in the climate crisis, it can be hard to know how to think about the future. Maybe things will only change a little bit. Maybe they'll change a lot. Some things may get better, and others worse. We have to acknowledge that things do not always go they way we plan. And that it will be OK.

THE LESS WE EXPECT TOMORROW TO BE THE SAME AS TODAY, THE LESS WE WILL BE FRIGHTENED OF THINGS CHANGING.

Not only do older people have the advantage of not having so much future ahead of them, but our life experiences often tell us that even really terrible difficulties can be overcome. Sometimes the thing you most dread actually happens, and sometimes you recover from it. But like any plant, however weather-resistant, it helps to have strong foundations, like good soil and water. So, let's use the tool kit on the next pages to lay the groundwork so that we can grow into the most resilient creatures we can be . . .

WHATEVER THE
FUTURE BRINGS, WE
CAN MEET IT WITH
AN OPEN MIND

Thought patterns to let go of

Here are some unhelpful habits that work against resilience and how we can reframe them to manage our eco-anxiety.

CATASTROPHIZING

This means thinking of the worst-case scenario and acting like it's definitely going to happen. Remember that not only do we not know what will happen in the future, but sometimes bad things happen and people respond beautifully.

HOPELESSNESS

This one's terrible as it has the double-whammy effect of making us sad in the present as well as making it less likely that we will try to make things better. Hope is necessary for change—keep yours alive and invest in a brighter future.

RUMINATIONS

Sometimes our thoughts get stuck in a loop. This tends to happen with problems we can't solve—we keep going back to them as if it will be different this time. But the thoughts you're having are already making a difference to how you act, and that's plenty for now.

RAGE

It's easy to feel angry when you think of the people who are harming the planet for profit. But our actions can be powered by love instead of hate, and doing so will allow us to welcome more people into the movement in the long term.

Five pillars of resilience

1 REST

It's much harder to regulate your moods when you're tired. Resting is also one of the most eco-friendly activities in the world, so do it as much as you need to.

2 HEALTH

Physical health is also very important for mood-regulation and energy levels. Even simple exercise, like going for a walk, can release happiness hormones into your system.

3 AGENCY

This means having the sense that the things you do can make a difference. Even if all you can do for now is to make small changes in your own life, that's wonderful. As you grow up you will begin to access more ways to act on Earth's behalf.

4 COMMUNITY

Having a network of friends and family is not only helpful for mental stability, but also for taking bigger actions and making more effective changes. And on that subject...

5 ACTIVE HOPE

Passive hope — crossing your fingers and hoping for the best — isn't going to solve the crisis. But active hope very well might! If we have the hope that we can make things better, then it will always seem worthwhile to keep trying.

⤳⤳ Step 9 ⤳⤳

Practice Self-care

HAVE YOU HEARD OF THE TERM "SELF-CARE"?

SELF-CARE IS ALL ABOUT LOOKING AFTER YOURSELF.

In the process of managing your eco-anxiety, you can lose sight of the things that make you happy and healthy. Self-care might take the form of enjoyable distractions or deep personal growth. Both are worthwhile, and looking after yourself is an important part of looking after others, too.

Have you ever heard the phrase, "You can't pour from an empty cup"?

This saying means that in order for us to effectively take care of others, we must first take care of ourselves. It's like when you're on an airplane and hear the flight attendants say, "In the event of an emergency, for parents traveling with small children, it's important that you put on your own oxygen mask first." They have to say this because this is the last thing most parents would ever think of doing. But it's vital that they get their own oxygen masks on quickly—because without oxygen they won't be physically capable of taking care of others. The reason I'm using this flight analogy is because when you become anxious about the state of the world it's easy to forget that you too are an important and precious part of it. Not only that, but we need you at your best so you can become part of the solution.

LOOKING AFTER YOURSELF IS A VITAL PART OF BEING THE BEST EARTH ALLY YOU CAN BE.

If you're drained of hope and energy, or if you don't like yourself very much, it can be tempting to give up — and I think we can all agree that this isn't a good idea. So, not only is it important to be real and let yourself feel the sadness, it's also important to top yourself up with happiness and energy — just like a planet-friendly refillable jar. **You may be asking at this point, is it even possible to feel good in the middle of a crisis? I'm here to tell you: Yes, it is.**

A couple of years ago I spoke to a doctor who works in Tasmania, a part of Australia that was particularly affected by wildfires in 2020. Not only were her patients stressed about climate change, so was she. She told me the only way she could cope was to practice "functional denial." This might sound a bit odd — isn't denial the thing we're meant to be fighting against? What she meant was that she had to switch off from the problem on a regular basis, otherwise she'd be overwhelmed. If she wanted to keep looking after her patients, she had to do things that helped her temporarily to forget what was going on.

Rather than thinking of it as completely pushing the problem out of your mind, maybe it's more helpful to imagine changing your focus. If you look closely at the palm of your hand, the rest of your surroundings goes fuzzy. You know they're still there, but you lose sight of everything else and get lost in the lines, the lumps and bumps, and maybe the way the light makes the skin shiny in places. It can be useful to shift your focus away from life's problems once in a while. The most important thing you need to know about the distraction, or functional denial, part of self-care is that it's for you, so only you have to like it.

It's all very well for people to tell you to meditate or do yoga, but what if you think that sounds a bit boring? Maybe you're the sort of person who prefers jumping on a trampoline or practicing ballet. Or perhaps you like making new playlists, doing origami, or baking cupcakes. You could be into literally anything! That's one of the things that's so brilliant about people — we're all different.

THE ONE STANDARDIZED THING YOU CAN SAY ABOUT SELF-CARE IS THAT IT NEEDS TO BE SOMETHING THAT REALLY AND TRULY TAKES YOUR MIND OFF THINGS.

Who knew that this could be a crucial part of caring for Earth? But it can! Nothing is too trivial or odd. It just has to work for you.

It probably goes without saying that some of the things we like might be bad for the planet, so these obviously aren't going to work as self-care activities. When we talk about functional denial, we mean a kind of temporary denial that helps to keep us functioning, but it also has to be "functional" in relation to the environment. Buying some fast fashion to take your mind off the emergency, for instance, would be better off being called "dysfunctional denial." And that's definitely no way to help. yourself feel better!

Self-care activities

Here are some self-care activites for very different types of people. I know you're unique, and not a "type" at all, but at least this might give you some ideas to start off with. Maybe you're even a little bit of each — in which case, mix it up!

SELF-CARE FOR EXTROVERTS

Talk to a friend. Talk to ten friends. Throw a party. Put on a funny outfit or even get a wild haircut so that everyone talks to you!

SELF-CARE FOR INTROVERTS

Read a book. Listen to a podcast. Decorate your room. Create artwork. Talk to a friend (Introverts have friends, too!).

SELF-CARE FOR SPORTY TYPES

Go for a walk, run, swim, or bike ride. Or maybe all four! See how many skips in a row you can do with a jump rope.

SELF-CARE FOR RELAXED TYPES

Get enough sleep. Take a long, hot bath. Watch a movie you liked when you were little, even if you've seen it a hundred times — or especially if you've seen it a hundred times!

SELF-CARE FOR CLEVER TYPES

Learn to write a few words in Sanskrit. Try to understand what Einstein was about. Study Greek myths. Find out what makes water wet.

Ways to cultivate your character

1 FRIENDLINESS

One terrifying myth about the future is that resources will become so scarce that humans will turn against one another to survive. But there is another future where people help one another. We can start that future now.

2 CURIOSITY

Curious people ask good questions and seek out good answers. In other words, they are problem-solvers and are open to new worlds and possibilities.

3 COURAGE

It goes without saying that moving into an uncertain future requires a huge amount of courage. A bit like functional denial, courage can involve temporarily pushing certain ideas out of your mind so you can do what needs to be done.

4 GRATITUDE

We live on a most extraordinary planet. And we live on it at a time when we are well-placed to understand its extraordinariness scientifically as well as intuitively.

5 CALM

Calm is perhaps the hardest quality to cultivate, but it rubs off on other people too, so it's worthwhile thinking about how to let go of your worries and just **BE** once in a while.

Connect with Nature

BEING CONNECTED WITH NATURE IS ABOUT FEELING CLOSE TO THE WIDER NATURAL WORLD.

IT'S A RELATIONSHIP THAT MAKES US FEEL GOOD.

We all have different experiences of nature and different reasons for wanting to connect with it. A strong connection with nature means feeling a close relationship to our surroundings. When you encounter nature, remind yourself that you are not a passive observer, but an active part of our natural world.

Nature has always been all around us.

Around two hundred and fifty years ago, during a time known as the Industrial Revolution (when people in Europe and the United States began to rely much more heavily on the use of machines and chemicals), people were conflicted about the purpose of nature. Was it a terrible, destructive force that needed to be controlled and tamed? Or was it a state of bliss that we needed to make our way back to? You could say, well, obviously the second one, but it turns out not to be so simple.

One of the problems with thinking of nature as intrinsically charming and good was that maybe it only looked that way to certain people because they were seeing it through the lens of culture. It was all very well for rich, white industrialists to sit in their stately homes, eating food made from the products of industrial agriculture, and moan about being disconnected from the natural world. But what if that was just their wealthy, white privilege speaking? They were able to seek the joys of nature while benefitting from the very industrialization that was destroying it.

This unfortunate history has left its mark on those who live in industrial societies, so much so that the only flower species some people see are the ones sold in the supermarket. These days, even if you live right in the middle of the countryside, your relationship with nature is likely to be affected by industrialization.

So where should you go to look for it? Can you find nature in a city park? A zoo? The rolling fields of a green and pleasant yet intensively farmed countryside? Or do you have to go to an ancient forest, or perhaps to the bottom of the ocean? And what will you do when you get there? Take a photo? Or wander about in dreamlike awe, stroking every leaf and waving at every unsuspecting creature?

Perhaps the main thing we need to truly understand about nature is that it's not a destination for us to go and visit: It's everywhere. Those of us who live in big cities might not feel like we encounter much wild foliage in our day-to-day lives, but even the air around us is part of the natural world. It moves and blows and dissipates, and if we fill it with toxic fumes, these will pollute the atmosphere. Even in the busiest city you can find animals in the early morning before the day's bustle begins. From bugs and birds to rabbits and rats, nature can be found in every nook and cranny. Even the weeds that grow up through our sidewalks or the bushes that line our streets are a part of nature.

NATURE HAS NO BORDERS. WE NEED TO LOVE IT WHEREVER WE FIND IT.

Nature is really good for us, too. Research suggests people with a greater connection to nature are more likely to be happier and behave positively toward the environment.

But connecting with nature doesn't mean having a special, isolated experience and then going back to your life. Nor does it have to mean living in a self-sufficient community. It means appreciating the world in its enormity and understanding that it forms one gigantic, staggering ecosystem.

If you are lucky enough to have seen a mountain range, rainforest, or wild beach, then you will know that being in unspoiled nature affects the way you think. It's so sublime and impressive it can make your own worries seem tiny. It's exciting to see rock formations, giant plants, or seals diving in the waves. Nature gives us so much to occupy our minds with — it's limitlessly fascinating and beautiful. Many towns and cities contain wonderful botanical gardens, tended according to natural principles, where you can really feel nature at work. Even in more heavily populated areas you can often find densely overgrown railway sidings or thriving patches of lush, untended foliage. If you look for nature in an open-minded way you will find it, and you won't have to go very far.

THE BEST THING YOU CAN DO FOR NATURE IS TO LOVE IT UNCONDITIONALLY, APPRECIATE IT CONCEPTUALLY, AND RESPECT IT ABSOLUTELY.

You can love nature whoever and wherever you are. You don't need money, you don't need transportation, and you don't need permission. All you need is compassion, understanding, and a big heart.

NATURE IS NOT
A PLACE TO VISIT.

IT IS HOME.

Ways to connect with nature

1 DISCOVER PLANTS ON YOUR DOORSTEP

All of nature is a marvel. It's every bit as incredible to see a dandelion or clover bursting though concrete as it is to see a forest.

2 LOOK OUT FOR EVERY CRITTER

Ecosystems don't run on cuteness. Every living creature is important, and even the most dangerous, stinky, or slimy animal has its place in the world.

3 LEARN ABOUT HUMAN HISTORY

If we're going to have a future where we prevent the mistakes of our past, we need to have an understanding of our history. Learn what you can about industrialization and globalization and see how they have shaped our world.

4 GET INTERESTED IN THE WEATHER

It's not only plants and animals that will determine our survival, but weather, too. Instead of just listening to the forecast, ask yourself what weather is. Why does the wind blow or the rain fall? All weather is beautiful!

5 THINK ABOUT SPACE

Sometimes life on Earth can seem completely overwhelming. When things down here are really getting to you, it can be such a relief to think about the universe. After all, in the grand scheme of things, the whole universe is nature.

Engaging with your senses

The Japanese have a term, shinrin yoku, which translates as "forest bathing." It means using your senses to engage with nature in order to feel its calming, therapeutic benefits.

SMELL

Enjoy the subtle smells of plants. It's not only roses that smell wonderful, even humble grasses or damp leaves have a delicious, soothing aroma.

TOUCH

Notice the different textures of plants. Some are stiff and shiny, while others are soft and hairy. Maybe lie on the ground and feel the solidity of the earth beneath you.

LOOK

Gaze up through the leaves to the sky. Perhaps take a close-up photograph showing the incredible detail in a tiny part of nature.

TASTE

If you're fortunate enough to have a family member with a good knowledge of edible plants, ask them to take you foraging. Perhaps you will find wild garlic, or nettles to make into tea.

LISTEN

Open your ears to the sounds of birds and insects, or the air moving through the leaves. No composer can compete with the sounds of the natural world!

We've been on quite a journey together throughout this book.

I feel privileged to have been given a space to put down some thoughts. I hope some of my thoughts have been helpful. They're not even solely *my* thoughts, really. They're a mixture of lots of people's thoughts all arranged together in one place. Take a moment to digest and acknowledge how you're feeling. When you turn the page, you'll find ideas on ways to express what eco-anxiety means to you.

I love to express my feelings through writing. When I wrote my first climate-related book thirty years ago, most of us thought that the environmental changes we feared were at least a few generations away. One of the biggest shocks has been how quickly small changes in planetary temperature make a huge difference to both weather systems and ecosystems.

I feel so sorry that my generation didn't do nearly enough. In a sense, climate change is both expected and unexpected. We saw it coming, and we didn't. Even now, we can't predict exactly how it's going to unfold. But it seems that you and I are likely to witness extraordinary events that will change the ways we think about the world and how we inhabit it. People all over the world are fighting hard to bring about changes that need to be made, and I know you will be part of that battle. But always remember that our strongest force is love. With all of our love, and the actions that spring from it, the future is bright.

Before you sit down to put pen to paper, or finger to keyboard, have a look back at some of the things you've learned. Maybe the main thing is never to feel alone with your fears. Since I've been researching the field of eco-anxiety, the thing I've probably read most often is that it helps to talk to other people about it. Sometimes even I find myself thinking, *What's the point?* But then I find myself having a really good chat with a friend (or sometimes a stranger), and it actually turns out to be true. **Talking about the climate emergency really, truly helps.** Sometimes it just helps you, sometimes it also helps the other person, and, if enough of us do it, it can also help the planet.

Then there's all the other stuff, like not being afraid to have feelings. Or trying not to let the size of the problem get to you. Or taking care of yourself and fostering your resilience. And above all, always letting your love for the planet guide your actions. There is a climate change activist named Aubrey Meyer whose work was nominated for the Nobel Peace Prize in 2008. He suggests we behave like musicians and start playing together harmoniously.

We need to think like an orchestra with all its different instruments: If enough of us start to play in tune and in time, we can make extraordinary things happen.

Creativity is a vital part of life. Art, music, and poetry aren't just luxuries for times when everything is going well. We need to know we can express ourselves at all times and in all situations. People have written beautiful poems on battlefields, in refugee camps, or while they were chronically ill. **Art never stops.**

Here are some ways to give form to your thoughts and feelings about climate change.

WRITE A POEM

Decide whether you want it to rhyme or not. It can be long or short, sad or celebratory. You could choose a plant or an animal as a theme, or just make it about your feelings.

WRITE A STORY

Your story can be imaginative or factual. It could be more like a fairy tale or a newspaper article. Of course, it can be sad or scary, but it could also be funny.

WRITE A SONG

It would be good if pop stars could be a bit more vocal about the climate. Maybe what the world needs is a hit record about the climate emergency. Written by you!

WRITE A JOURNAL

Keeping a journal is a great way to organize your thoughts and feelings. You can say whatever you like without worrying about what anyone else will think.

WRITE A LETTER

It could be to a friend or someone you admire. Perhaps it could be a thank-you letter for something they've done for the climate.

To say farewell, I've written a haiku just for you. A haiku is a Japanese poetry style with seventeen syllables, set in three lines of five, seven, and five syllables. They traditionally evoke images of the natural world. Mine's titled "Leaves." I hope you enjoy it and close this book feeling inspired to write your own.

Leaves

I HEARD A RUSTLE.

THE FUTURE WAS WHISPERING,

"PLEASE COME AND JOIN ME."

ACTIVISM — the actions people take to make the changes they want to see in the world.

AGENCY — the ability to take action or choose what action to take.

CARBON-NEUTRAL — not increasing the amount of carbon dioxide in Earth's atmosphere.

CATASTROPHIZE — to imagine the worst possible outcome.

CLIMATE CHANGE — changes in Earth's climate, especially the gradual rise in temperature caused by high levels of carbon dioxide.

CLIMATE DENIAL — refusing to accept that climate change is happening.

COGNITIVE DISSONANCE — anxiety that results from simultaneously holding contradictory attitudes or beliefs.

COLLECTIVE ACTION — action taken together by a group of people who aim to achieve a common objective.

CONTRADICTION — a situation where two or more ideas are in opposition to one another.

COPING MECHANISM — something a person does to deal with a difficult situation.

DEFEATIST — someone who thinks or talks in a way that suggests they expect to be unsuccessful.

ECO-ANXIETY — a state of distress caused by concern about damage to the environment.

ECOLOGICAL THOUGHT — the idea of interconnectedness.

ECOSYSTEM — all the plants and animals that live in a particular area together with the complex relationship that exists between them and their environment.

EMISSION — a substance that is produced and sent out into the air. Some are harmful to the environment, especially carbon dioxide or methane.

EXTROVERT — a socially confident person.

FAST FASHION — the reproduction of clothes at high speed and low cost. These clothes are often worn once and then thrown away.

FLEXITARIANISM — a diet centered on plant foods with the occasional inclusion of meat or fish.

FORAGING — finding food by hunting, fishing, or gathering.

FOSSIL FUELS — fuels such as coal and oil that are formed from decayed plant or animal remains.

GLOBALIZATION — the process by which the world is becoming interconnected because of increased trade and cultural exchange.

GLOBAL NORTH — the richest and most industrialized countries, which are mainly in the northern part of the world.

INDUSTRIALIZATION — the shift away from agriculture toward manufactured goods, which are often produced by machines.

INNER CRITIC — a negative internal voice.

JARGON — special words or phrases that are used by particular groups of people, especially in their work.

MISINFORMATION — the spreading of false ideas.

OPTIMISM — the tendency to see the good side of things or to expect the best in any situation.

PARASYMPATHETIC NERVOUS SYSTEM — a network of nerves that relaxes your body after periods of stress or danger.

PESSIMISM — the tendency to see the bad side of things or to expect the worst in any situation.

RENEWABLE ENERGY — energy produced from sources like the sun and wind that are naturally replenished and do not run out.

REWILDING — the practice of returning areas of land to a wild state, including the reintroduction of animal species.

RUMINATION — obsessive repetition of thoughts.

SAFE SPACE — a place where people can gather free from discrimination or harrassment

SELF-CARE — the practice of looking after one's own well-being

SPECIES — a set of animals or plants in which the members have similar characteristics to one another and can breed with one another.

SUSTAINABLE — causing little or no damage to the environment and therefore able to continue for a long time.

SYMPATHETIC NERVOUS SYSTEM — a network of nerves that helps your body activate its fight-or-flight response.

TIPPING POINT — the point at which a series of small changes or incidents becomes significant enough to cause a larger change.

VALIDATION — recognition or affirmation that a person or their feelings or opinions are valid or worthwhile.

Find out more about the climate crisis and ways to deal with eco-anxiety with the help of an adult.

BOOKS

Generation Green by Linda Sivertsen

How You Can Save the Planet by Hendrikus van Hensbergen

No One is Too Small to Make a Difference by Greta Thunberg

We Have a Dream by Mya-Rose Craig and illustrated by Sabrena Khadija

PODCASTS

The Big Melt from Earth Rangers/Gen-Z Media
An engaging discussion of questions about climate change

"Episode 1: Tipping Points"

Climate Crisis Conversations from the Climate Psychology Alliance
Thoughtful conversations between climate psychologists about the climate crisis

"Episode 5: Deep Questioning: Navigating Youth at a Time of Climate Change"

WEBSITES

American Museum of Natural History
Climate change information and activities, including games, quizzes, and videos

amnh.org/explore/ology/climate-change

BBC Children in Need
Well-being advice and resources for eco-anxiety

bbcchildreninneed.co.uk/changing-lives/understanding-the-climate-crisis-and-eco-anxiety

Climate Change Resources
News, resources, and climate change facts for teens and kids

climatechangeresources.org/youth